CURTIS INTERNATIONAL
PORTRAITS OF GREATNESS

•

General Editor
Enzo Orlandi

Text by
Liana Bortolon

Translator
C. J. Richards

Published by
ARNOLDO MONDADORI EDITORE
and
THE CURTIS PUBLISHING COMPANY

THE
LIFE
&
TIMES
OF
LEONARDO

CURTIS BOOKS
A division of
The Curtis Publishing Company
Philadelphia • New York

IN SEARCH OF
THE IMPOSSIBLE

This is the earliest known drawing by Leonardo. It is dated August 5, 1473, and now hangs in the Uffizi Gallery in Florence. The landscape, drawn in great detail, shows the valley of the Arno and Montelupo Castle. These were his childhood haunts, lovingly explored during long rambles in the hills, when Leonardo was still living with his father's family: his stepmother, his paternal grandparents and his uncle Francesco, his first playmate. In the photograph at the top: The house where

Leonardo was born as it is today, in Anchiano near Vinci in the lower valley of the Arno, dominated by a great plain that stretches to the Apennine Mountains. From his childhood Leonardo showed a passionate interest in things; he collected everything, from small animals to flowers, from leaves to oddly shaped pieces of wood. After his stepmother's death, in 1465 (his first great loss), Leonardo went to Florence with his father.

"We should not desire the impossible . . ." advised Leonardo in one of his notebooks. The admonition was probably aimed at himself, a reminder to stay within the bounds of reality and to preserve a sense of measure. The world has seen how many of his discoveries were rediscovered by later scientists, how many of his dreams were realized. In the eyes of his contemporaries, however, Leonardo must have seemed, with his active imagination and with his clever prophetic thinking, a man who sought the impossible. This universal genius, who proved himself in every field, has left almost no trace of his private life. "The events of my life are my thoughts," say his papers. Even the date of his birth, April 15, 1452, at three o'clock on a Saturday morning, was ascertained only a few years ago by a scholar, Emile Moeller, who came upon it in a page of the diary of Ser Antonio, Leonardo's grandfather, in the archives of Florence. The artist was born at Anchiano near Vinci, the son of a local notary, Ser Piero, and of a peasant girl, Caterina, who later married Accattabriga del Vacca. When the child was five he went to live in his father's house. His father had, meantime, married a sixteen-year-old girl of a good family, Albiera Amadori. She remained childless and lavished her affection on Leonardo. However, Albiera died young, and Ser Piero remarried three times. Leonardo probably lived in Vinci until he was fourteen.

Later he was to remember only two incidents of this period. The first one he interpreted as a prophecy. He was still in his cradle when a kite plummeted down on him. He opened his mouth, and its tail hit him several times between the lips. He was to interpret the second recollection as a symbol of his fate. When he was a little older, he found himself one day at the entrance of a cave in the Apennines. Overcoming his fear of the dark, mysterious cavern, he ventured inside, prompted "by the burning desire to see whether there might be any marvelous thing within." It was that "burning desire," that unquenchable curiosity, that became the secret spring of his life.

When he arrived in Florence,
Leonardo was already an
extremely handsome young man.
Blond, with piercing blue eyes and
a tall slender frame, he must
have been very like·the shepherd
in the "Adoration of the Magi,"
which is popularly believed
to be a self-portrait (enlargement
at left). The same face, the
same features can be recognized
in Verrocchio's "David" (above),
which appears to be a portrait by
the master of the young pupil
who had recently come to his shop.

5

AN UNQUENCHABLE THIRST FOR KNOWLEDGE

To learn, to know, were Leonardo's goals in life from his very infancy. He was attracted to knowledge as are others to art or to faith. "Everywhere, his mind turned to difficult matters," wrote Vasari. This thirst carried Leonardo to the threshold of the "impossible." Every time he undertook a new project he started from scratch, building by his own methods a body of knowledge from which to move forward—from the technique of fresco painting to the manufacture of tools. This approach met with numerous failures and endless criticism. But genius, to achieve its potential, must be put to use. Therefore Leonardo placed himself at the service of some of the rulers of the period. During the years he spent in Milan (from 1482 to 1500) in the service of Ludovico il Moro he studied all manner of subjects: the canalization of rivers, the making of engines of war, the architecture of churches and of civic buildings, music and even theatrical costuming. In 1502, after he had left Milan and had been appointed "architect and military engineer" by Cesare Borgia, he turned his attention to fortifications. When the Venetian Republic was threatened by the Turks, he drew up a system of defense based on diverting the Isonzo River. Later he did the same for the Arno River to defend the Florentine Republic, which was at war with Pisa. In Rome, under the patronage of Giuliano de Medici, he turned his attention to the study of anatomy, and made plans for the reclamation of the Pontine marshes. For Charles d'Amboise, the representative of the King of France in Milan, he designed a modern and comfortable residence. It also seems that, at the invitation of the Egyptian Diodario, the Sultan's representative, he made or at least imagined and described a trip to the Near East to study the region of the Caucasus. Sometimes the faith placed in him by his patrons changed into open distrust when they were confronted with his failures—programs that were too ambitious for the times. These resulted in bitterness and misunderstanding. Undoubtedly the most serene years of his life were the last three, from 1516 to 1519, when, having accepted the hospitality of his great admirer, King Francis I, he lived at the Castle of Cloux. Here, respected and admired, he was able to pursue his studies in every field. On May 12, 1519, at 67, the elderly sage died in the arms of his faithful disciple, Francesco Melzi.

Even as an old man, Leonardo must have presented a noble, awe-inspiring appearance as revealed in the self-portrait, in red chalk, upper left. It is also generally believed that Raphael portrayed him in his priestly figure of Plato (lower left) in the fresco of the "School of Athens" in the Vatican. The two artists probably met in Florence at the time of the "Battle of Anghiari" and perhaps also in Rome. The intense look, the long hair and the beard all contribute to create an impression of asceticism. The "Medusa," below (at the Uffizi Gallery), was probably inspired by a very youthful work of

Leonardo's. One day a peasant gave Leonardo's father a round wooden panel and asked him to have it decorated. Ser Piero asked his son to do so. The result—a mass of snakes and lizards all spitting fire—was so terrifying that Ser Piero himself was badly frightened. Realizing it would never do for the peasant, but being a shrewd businessman, he sold it to a Florentine art dealer for 100 ducats. The latter did even better by selling it to the Duke of Milan for 300. Meantime Ser Piero had bought another wood panel showing a heart pierced by an arrow, which he gave to the delighted peasant.

When Leonardo was a child he used to draw everything he saw during his trips through the countryside. Aware of his son's interests and activities, Ser Piero apprenticed him to Andrea Verrocchio (*Andrea di Cione*) so that he might perfect his skill and develop his talent. In Verrocchio's workshop were other pupils who later became famous. Leonardo's first work was the angel holding a mantle in the famous "Baptism of Christ" by Verrocchio (at the Uffizi). The hand of the teacher is evident in the whole composition (*reproduced at the left*); but the figure of the kneeling angel already shows glimpses of the characteristics of Leonardo's art. We need only look closely at the detail shown on the page at the right: The foreshortening of the head, the luminous, light, tumbling hair, the sweetness and brightness of the eyes—all these will be found again in the works of his maturity. Leonardo was 23 when he painted this angel. "Although he was very young," Vasari wrote, "Leonardo did it in such a way that his angel was much better than the figures Andrea painted; it was for this reason that Andrea never again wanted to touch paints, humiliated that a youth should have been better than he." A radiogram of the painting shows that the first sketching in of the master's angel was quite different from the pupil's. Therefore the latter had already freed himself from Verrocchio's influence and justified what Vasari wrote.

A GIFTED APPRENTICE

Left: Two profiles of warriors. *The first one belongs to the statue of Bartolomeo Colleoni, by Verrocchio; the second one, a silver point drawing by Leonardo (at the British Museum) was inspired by a bas-relief of the master. There is a remarkable similarity between the figures despite the dissimilarity of the materials used.*

Leonardo entered Verrocchio's workshop when he was fourteen. It was at this time that his father, whose first wife had died in 1465, moved to Florence with his family. Verrocchio, who was then in his thirties, was considered by his contemporaries to be the best painter, sculptor, and goldsmith of the period. He had studied sculpture under Donatello and painting under Pesellino and Alessio Baldovinetti. His workshop was frequented by the most promising young men of the time: Botticelli, who was then twenty-three, Perugino, twenty, Lorenzo di Credi, fourteen, and many others. Leonardo immediately felt at home. The apprentices worked in groups so that it is difficult to determine exactly what each one contributed to the paintings that came out of the master's shop. However, we do know that the angel holding up the drapery in the Baptism of Christ is entirely Leonardo's work. After six years of apprenticeship, da Vinci was admitted into the corporation of San Luca, the Florentine guild of artists. His first known drawing bears the date August 5, 1473. Except for the influence of Verrocchio whom, in any event, he surpassed within a few years, it cannot be said that Leonardo owes anything to his contemporaries. His style very soon freed itself from the gracefulness and love of detail that was characteristic of the Renaissance, and he began to tackle more complex problems—like that of light—which prefigured baroque painting. This did not affect Leonardo's deep affection for Verrocchio. On the contrary, he continued to live in his house even after his father had rented a studio for him. He did, however, learn technique from Verrocchio. For example, there is a silver point drawing by Leonardo, dated 1480, copied from a bas-relief by the master, that is reminiscent of the monument to Bartolomeo Colleoni. In all other matters, Leonardo was self-taught. "In erudition and especially in literature he would have derived great profit," comments Vasari, "if he had not been so changeable and unstable. He started to learn many things and then, when they were begun, he gave them up."

Above, in bas-relief, two other profiles of warriors with sumptuous helmets, which Leonardo must have seen, probably during his first Florentine period. Top: a ceramic warrior from the famous shop of the Della Robbia family. Below it: imaginary portrait of Alexander the Great by Verrocchio. In Leonardo's day finely wrought arms and armor were produced in the workshop of Verrocchio. He was considered an outstanding goldsmith and had a first-class clientele.

TWO YOUTHFUL ANNUNCIATIONS

Of Leonardo's youthful works, two "Annunciations" remain. One is now at the Uffizi, the other at the Louvre. The first one is a large wood panel (seven feet by three feet) which reflects the Renaissance style then in vogue. For a long time it was attributed to Ghirlandaio, among others. The marble sarcophagus which divides the composition in two was copied from Piero de Medici's tomb, which Verrocchio had carved in the old sacristy of the church of San Lorenzo. The second one is a small predella which belonged to an altarpiece painted by Lorenzo di Credi for the Cathedral in Pistoia. During that period—between 1475 and 1478—Leonardo came into contact with Lorenzo the Magnificent, who arranged to have him work in the garden of San Marco in Florence. Ser Piero undoubtedly had a hand in this arrangement for, although he allowed his son independence, he did not lose sight of him. Again it was Leonardo's father who obtained him a commission, in January, 1478, for a painting destined for the Chapel of St. Bernard in the Signory Palace. Leonardo received an advance of 22 florins, but he never did the work. Instead, he painted, in September, two Virgin Marys which have since become known as the "Benois Madonna," now at the Hermitage in Leningrad, and the "Madonna of the Cat," of which only drawings now remain. In 1478 he was also commissioned to prepare a cartoon for the King of Portugal for a tapestry of the story of Adam and Eve.

*Above: This beautiful
"Annunciation," in the Uffizi, was
painted by the young Leonardo when
he was still in Verrocchio's shop.
The predella on the same subject
(lower left), done shortly before
this, was painted for Lorenzo di
Credi's "Madonna di Piazza"
(at the Louvre). It is a small piece,
but of exquisite workmanship.
Left: An elegant study of the
drapery on the arm of the angel
in the first "Annunciation."
It is one of the few drawings of
da Vinci that can positively
be identified as a work
of his youth.*

13

The "Adoration of the Magi," reproduced below, which measures nine feet by eight feet, is at the Uffizi. Vasari saw it in 1568 at the house of Amerigo de Benci. The painting was not finished because of Leonardo's departure from Florence. Fifteen years later, the monks of San Donato a Scopeto substituted for it a painting on the same subject by Filippo Lippi.

Leonardo made a great number of preparatory sketches and drawings for this "Adoration." The drawing, at the right, which is at the Louvre, shows how the figures of the kneeling wise men were studied before they were covered with rich clothing. On the opposite page, a complete architectural study of the background.

A PERIOD OF CRISIS

Leonardo went through a period of crisis after he left Verrocchio's workshop. On the one hand, his spirit, which had been in close touch with the humanistic culture of Florence, was evolving, forcing him to make a total reappraisal of his ideas. On the other hand, although he felt called to a high mission, he had no money to meet the challenge—sometimes not even enough to buy paints.

Since 1480, the artist's name had not figured in Ser Piero's tax books, so he undoubtedly was no longer being supported by his father. Nonetheless, Ser Piero continued to extend his paternal protection by securing a commission for his son. In August, 1481, Leonardo contracted with the monks of San Donato a Scopeto to do an altarpiece for them. This "Adoration of the Magi" was his first large work. He threw himself into the project with great

enthusiasm, working up its composition in a series of sketches. (It is to this altarpiece that we owe the only self-portrait of the young Leonardo. He is the shepherd at the right.) But this cannot have been a very remunerative occupation.

Leonardo was waiting for his great chance; it came to him at the end of 1482. Having learned that the artist had made a silver lyre in the shape of a horse's skull, Lorenzo the Magnificent decided to send the lyre and its maker to Ludovico il Moro, the new lord of Milan, as a gesture of friendship. Abandoning the "Adoration of the Magi," which was only half finished, Leonardo agreed to go. He was accompanied by a singer, Atalante Miglioretti, and by Tomaso da Peretola, nicknamed Zoroastro.

"THE MEDICI MADE ME AND THE MEDICI DESTROYED ME"

The drawing of a Madonna (lower left), belonging to the Uffizi, is one of the most interesting and complete sketches by Leonardo. Note the elegant lines based on geometric figures—ellipses and triangles—in which are enclosed the figures of Mary and the Child. Next to this is one of the studies done for the "Madonna of the Cat." This drawing is in the British Museum. The composition is completed with an arch similar to the one in the "Madonna of the Cat" discovered in Savona, which some critics think is an original work of Leonardo. On the page to the right are reproductions of the four Madonnas that belong to the period of Leonardo's youth. At the top, the "Madonna of the Carnation," in the Munich Museum, and the "Madonna of the Flower," better known as the "Benois Madonna," in the Hermitage. Below left: The "Madonna of the Cat," in the collection of Carlo Noya in Savona, attributed, after skillful restoration, to da Vinci. Next to this is the "Litta Madonna," which is also at the Hermitage. It takes its name from the Litta family in Milan, to whom it belonged for a time.

In his youth Leonardo, like so many artists of the era, was fascinated by the image of the Virgin Mary. He often depicted her as a fragile adolescent without a halo, with the Christ child busily playing in her lap. However, these are works of such a little-known period in his life that it has been difficult to trace out their history with any certainty. The authenticity of the four Madonnas reproduced on the next page is, therefore, open to question. The "Madonna of the Carnation," for example, can probably be identified with the "Madonna of the Vase," which belonged to Pope Clement VII and which Vasari describes. The "Benois Madonna" is almost certainly one of the "Virgin Marys" which Leonardo painted in 1478. As for the "Madonna of the Cat," painted perhaps in the same year, it was thought to have been lost and only the numerous preparatory drawings for it remained. In the late 1930's, a Savona industrialist believed he recognized in one of these drawings a startling resemblance to a wood panel in his possession, painted by an unknown artist. Some scholars maintained that it was actually the original painted by Leonardo. The "Litta Madonna" was probably the one that was noticed in 1543 in the house of Michiel Contarini in Venice and was later in the Litta house in Milan until Czar Alexander II acquired it for the Hermitage. Even though it is not signed, it is traditionally attributed to Leonardo. All these figures, which have in common special grace and a sense of happy motherhood, seem to exude Leonardo's youthful zest. A handsome youth, an accomplished horseman, an admirable lute-player, an extemporaneous rhymester, Leonardo was a great asset to any form of festivity and "was so charming in his conversation," said Vasari, "that he drew people's hearts to himself." In the company of Leon Battista Alberti, he often took part in learned and philosophical discussions at Careggi, the villa of Piero de Medici, the wealthiest man in Florence. It was perhaps these gatherings which brought on Leonardo's crisis. In the margin of one of his notebooks he wrote the cryptic sentence: "The Medici made me and the Medici destroyed me."

Left: Two versions by Leonardo of the famous "Virgin of the Rocks." The one at the left is in the National Gallery in London; the one at the far left is at the Louvre. On April 25, 1483, Leonardo contracted, in collaboration with the De Predis brothers, to deliver, before December 8, an altarpiece for the Chapel of the Conception in the Church of San Francesco in Milan. As usual, Leonardo was distracted by other studies and did not finish the work on time. Consequently a suit was brought which dragged along for a quarter of a century. According to the art critics who made a thorough study of the problem, the first version, which was entirely Leonardo's, is the one at the Louvre. The other, which bears traces of collaboration with the De Predis brothers, is in London. The same subject was taken up again and again by pupils of Leonardo. The two small reproductions above are from this school: The one to the left is in the Church of Affori, near Milan; the other is in the Milan Picture Gallery.

WINGS, WATER, AND LIGHT

Angels, celestial creatures akin to birds, fascinated Leonardo. He gave his angels beautiful traits. He made them real beings, with somewhat disquieting features—a feminine grace and a melting expression. Their clothes are blown by the wind, their wings feathered and gigantic. Indeed, Leonardo was attracted by everything in the sky, from stars to birds to winged insects. "He often passed through places where birds are sold," Vasari noted, "and took them out of their cages with his hands, paying the vendors the price demanded, then let them fly away, giving them back their lost freedom." Perhaps he also wanted to study their flight.

At the same time Leonardo, with the patience and meticulousness of a scientist, imprisoned flies so that he might study the variations in their buzzing. One day he tried trimming the wings of some that were shut up in a box and were buzzing loudly. Then he put a bit of honey on their wings, thus obtaining different sounds. "You will note that by trimming those wings a bit," he wrote in his notebooks, "or better still, by lightly coating them with enough honey to prevent their flying, that their wings make a muffled noise as they flap, and the quality of the sound will go from a sharp note to a deep one in direct porportion to the extent that the free use of their wings has been curtailed." Every type of experiment set his mind working. In order to study the transmission of sound in water, he would spend long hours on the banks of a river with his ear at the end of a tube submerged in the water. He also made a number of experiments in the field of optics. These enabled him to develop scientifically that knowledge of the play of lights and shadows (chiaroscuro) and that misty quality (sfumato) that were to be the glory of his painting and the starting point of all the art that was to follow him. "Bathing objects in light is merging them with the infinite," said Leonardo. His principal debtor was Caravaggio as well as the long line of imitators of Caravaggio whose inspiration actually stemmed from Leonardo.

Opposite page: The angel of the "Annunciation," which was originally acquired by the Uffizi as a work of Ghirlandaio. The angel, in profile, raises one hand in blessing; in the other he holds a lily. This figure, although it is a link with classical iconography, already reveals the characteristics of Leonardo's art. Although his predecessors had given angels an ideal, superhuman aspect, da Vinci painted them as splendid creatures of this earth. Above: The angel of the "Madonna of the Rocks." It is the most suggestive of the ones done by da Vinci and the most expressive of his now mature art. Note the modeling of the head, the sweet and melancholy expression, the long elegant hand pointing to the Child. A study for this hand is in the Windsor collection. Hands, as we shall see, were of the utmost importance in Leonardo's painting.

A TASTE FOR
THE GROTESQUE

Beside the sweet faces
of angels and
madonnas, caricatures
are an unexpected and
surprising aspect of Leonardo's
art. This, however,
is merely another expression of
the same eagerness to know
and depict everything.
In Milan, Leonardo
was accustomed to
wander about with his
pad and pencil in
the most wretched
quarters of the city in order
to sketch portraits
of grotesque types
like the ones above (in
the Windsor collection)
and the ones to the right
(in the Milan Picture Gallery).

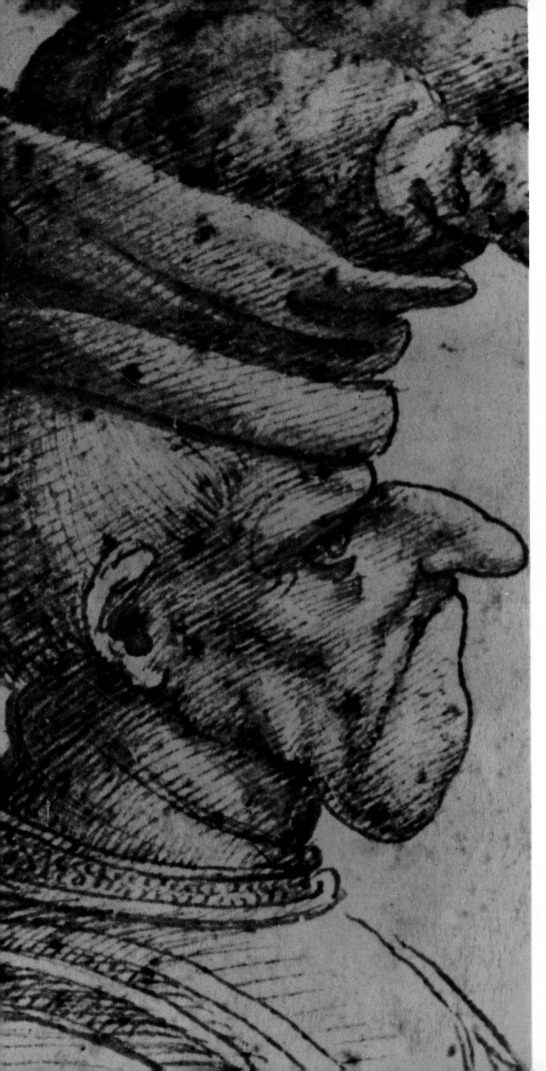

Two more studies of grotesque
expressions. The one to the left,
at the Ambrosiana, is at the
beginning of one of those satirical
fables with a moral in which
Leonardo made fun of fools. The
other, one of a series of studies of
expressions, is in Venice, at the
Academy. Leonardo always enjoyed
pranks. One day in Rome, where he
was living under the patronage of
Giuliano de Medici, he entertained
some visitors by blowing up the
entrails of a large ram with bellows.
As they were inflated they uncannily
started to float through the door
of the adjoining room, where the
assembled guests flattened
themselves in terror against the
wall to get away from the
creeping, transparent monster.

THE MIRACLE OF
THE LAST SUPPER

For three years, from 1495 to 1497, Leonardo worked on the "Last Supper," which he had undertaken to paint for the fathers of the Monastery of Santa Maria delle Grazie in Milan. This commission came at just the right moment, for the artist was going through a period of depression. When King Charles VIII descended on Italy at the head of a large army, the Duke was forced to forego the pleasures of art to arm his troops and to assign seven quintals of bronze, that were to have served for the monument to Francesco Sforza, to the army. Leonardo's disappointment must have been great, for he had already made numerous sketches for the statue. In a letter to his patron he wrote resentfully, "For thirty-six months I have had six mouths to feed, and in all I have received only fifty ducats." He was therefore glad to accept the commission. Many people came to watch him at work: princes of the church, the Duke himself, his courtiers, foreigners, artists. One day the old Cardinal of Gurk asked him if he was well paid. "Two thousand ducats a year, not counting presents and favors from the Duke," replied Leonardo, angry at the condescension and preferring to cover bitterness with irony. He wanted no pity.

"The Last Supper" as it appears today after its most recent and best restoration to date. This was undertaken to repair the damages suffered during World War II. The fresco had already been restored numerous times over the centuries, not always very skillfully. The chromatic pigment used by Leonardo had soon dissolved. Vasari, in his day, had seen nothing to worry about. On the wall opposite the "Last Supper" there was a fresco of a "Crucifixion" by Montorfano. Leonardo was to have painted over it also, but actually he confined himself to adding to the fresco tempera portraits of Ludovico il Moro and his consort, Beatrice d'Este, which were soon damaged. Today hardly a trace of these remains.

The pastel study for the head of the Redeemer, reproduced on the opposite page, which is in the Brera Picture Gallery, is usually attributed to Leonardo. The whole composition of the "Last Supper" measures approximately 30 feet by 14 feet. In 1498, Luca Pacioli, a great friend of da Vinci, spoke of it as of a work already finished. It is certain, however, that the heads of the Redeemer and Judas gave Leonardo a great deal of trouble; he never found models that were sufficiently sublime or expressive for the two principal characters. Some have seen in the head of Judas a certain resemblance to Savonarola, who was then a dominant figure in Florence.

A VINEYARD
IN SAN VITTORE

Although the "Last Supper" cost Leonardo three years of work, it won back the patronage of the Duke, who gave him, in the summer of 1498, "a vineyard and a piece of property of 16 rods" in the neighborhood of San Vittore. The following year the artist entrusted 600 ducats to a friend to deposit in his name at Santa Maria Novella in Florence. At the same time he was supporting his "family," that is, his pupils Salaino, Boltraffio and Marco d'Oggiono, an unknown man, and a servant girl named Caterina. As for himself, he made do with very little. He was a vegetarian who ate sparingly and drank with moderation because, he said, "wine gets even with the drinker." During these years Leonardo did a little bit of everything: catapults and fortifications, projects for the Cathedrals of Milan and Pavia, city planning, studies on flight. In order to get himself out of bed in the morning he made an alarm clock that was worked by water. He decorated the Sala delle Assi in the Sforza castle. But the golden days of the Sforza court had passed. The memory of the marriage celebrations for Beatrice d'Este and Isabella of Aragon had long since faded. Leonardo had served as director, costume master and scene designer for these weddings. When Ludovico's young wife died in 1496, the Duke had lost his zest for living. Besides, the threat of war with the French hung over him.

The "Last Supper" was preceded by a long series of preparatory drawings which are today in various collections: at the Ambrosiana in Milan, at the Louvre, at Windsor, at the Academy in Venice and at the Albertine Museum in Vienna. Leonardo traced, one by one, the figures of the Apostles, first without clothes so as to study closely their positions and movements; then in groups with ample robes. This was done to enable him to give rhythm to the composition and to put it together in a geometric design. He even jotted down the weights of the figures.

The figures which gave Leonardo the greatest trouble, as has already been noted, were those of Christ and Judas, so much so that while the work was in progress, the prior of the convent, Vincenzo Bandello, went to the Duke to complain because they had not yet been sketched. "Perhaps the fathers know how to paint?" retorted Leonardo to Ludovico who was questioning him. "How can they judge an artistic creation? Every day I devote two hours to this work." "How can that be if you never go there?" Ludovico said. "For one whole year I have gone every day, morning and evening, to the Borghetto, where the scum of humanity live, to find a face that will express the villainy of Judas, and I have not yet found it," Leonardo said. Then he added ironically, "Perhaps I could take as a model the prior who has been complaining about me to your Excellency; but I should not like to make him a laughingstock in his own convent." With this exchange, Leonardo continued his work at the pace he considered right for his artistic creation. In the three lunettes of the vaulted ceiling of the refectory of the church he painted an elegant mural decoration—a series of Sforza coats of arms and garlands.

On these two pages: Some of Leonardo's female heads and figures. In contrast to their opulent forms, their faces seem young. Their eyes, either modestly lowered or luminous and clear, lend a sweet, sad grace to their virginal expressions. Da Vinci drew their hairdos in minute detail as in the study (on this page, to the right) for the "Leda" (in Milan's Picture Gallery). On the opposite page, the "Leda" in the Gallotti Spiridon collection. Below: An angel's head for the "Virgin of the Rocks" at the Royal Palace in Turin. Bottom: Head of a woman (at Windsor) whose ghost of a smile foreshadows the "Mona Lisa's."

Even if Leonardo never married, was he susceptible to female charms? Looking at the women he painted, one would be inclined to say "yes." They are the most beautiful—certainly the most immortal, like the Mona Lisa—in the history of painting. And yet, women seem to have left no trace in Leonardo's private life. It is probable that Isabella d'Este exerted a spiritual fascination on him, as he did on her. In his diaries a certain Caterina crops up. She arrived in Milan in 1493 and figures among his "mouths to feed." Two years later, with his customary precision, he recorded the expenses incurred for her burial. They were rather high: "Three pounds of wax, twenty-seven soldi; coffin, eight soldi; canopy for the tomb, twelve soldi; transportation and setting up of a cross, four soldi; pallbearers, eight soldi; four priests and four minor clerics, twenty soldi; bells, books and sponges, two soldi; gravediggers, sixteen soldi; to the parish, eight soldi; permit, one soldo; sugar and candles, twelve soldi: total 118 soldi."

So large an expenditure for a simple servant girl seems excessive. Some have even thought that the Caterina in question was Leonardo's mother.

A DEVIL
IN ANGEL'S CLOTHES

As he had no family of his own, Leonardo adopted a little peasant boy from Oreno. Leonardo had met him in the country one day when the boy was making a charcoal drawing of his sheep on a stone. He had masses of blond curls, blue eyes and the clear rosy complexion characteristic of so many Lombards; he was as beautiful as a Leonardo drawing. The artist adopted him with a minimum of formalities, and took him to the castle of the Sforzas. Thieving, lying, and greedy, this angel of beauty did not, unhappily, live up to his looks. He betrayed his black soul so quickly that his name, Giacomo Caprotti, became Salai or Salaino, which means devil. Leonardo committed every sort of folly for him. Although he was normally economical, during the space of one year he bought for his protégé twenty-four pairs of shoes and at the same time, a cloak, a lined jerkin, 4 pairs of breeches and 3 coats. But Salaino continually stole from his adopted father and Leonardo, baffled, wrote in his notebooks: "I cannot get him to confess although I am certain he is guilty." When he was taken into town for dinner, Salaino ate enough for two and stole for four. At the tournament at the palace of Galeazzo di Sanseverino, while Leonardo was helping with the fitting of the costumes, the boy slipped into the men's dressing room, rifled the pockets and emptied the purses. Leonardo, instead of beating him roundly, showered him with gifts. As soon as he could afford it he had a splendid coat of silver cloth lined with velvet made for him. Salaino, who was then seventeen, showed it off delightedly.

Meantime Salaino had learned to paint and ended up by becoming his trusted companion. He followed him like a shadow for twenty-six years and left him only on the eve of his last trip, to the court of Francis I. A younger pupil, Francesco Melzi, was to inherit all Leonardo's drawings and manuscripts, but Salaino was remembered in his will. Leonardo's feelings toward his scoundrel of a pupil have been adjudged those of a perhaps too indulgent father. He was sufficiently patient and persistent with his adopted son to reform him at last and to make of him a quite competent artist.

There are many drawings that attest to the fascination which the beauty of adolescents exerted on Leonardo. In the first one, to the left, the classically perfect profile of his pupil, Salaino; next to it, the disheveled head of a youth not unlike the first one (both drawings are at Windsor). Below, another drawing inspired by Salaino, which is at the Louvre. On the opposite page, a sketch of Salaino in the costume he wore for his part in the "paradise festival," given on January 13, 1490, on the occasion of the marriage of Gian Galeazzo Sforza to Isabella of Aragon. Leonardo became reconciled with the Duke at this time and went to live in the castle.

THE RIDDLE OF THE MONA LISA

There have been many imitations and interpretations of the "Mona Lisa," beginning even before Leonardo had finished the painting. There is a veiled Mona Lisa at the Prado. There are also other versions, less chaste ones, like these pictures entitled "Nude Monna Vanna." They were all done in the 16th century except the one at the top, which dates from the 17th century. Leonardo's

When the Sforzas fell, Leonardo returned to Florence for a few years. Around 1503, according to Vasari, da Vinci was commissioned by a rich Florentine, Francesco del Giocondo, to do a portrait of his young and beautiful wife, Mona Lisa. "But, having worked at it for four years, he left it unfinished," commented his pessimistic biographer. Indeed, Leonardo must have considered the portrait unfinished because he took it with him to France, with other works, instead of sending it to the man who had commissioned it and presumably paid for it. This opens the thorny question of the "Mona Lisa" or the "Gioconda." Is it really the portrait of the 26-year-old consort of Francesco del Giocondo? Adolfo Venturi asserts that the lady portrayed is Costanza d'Avalos, Duchess of Francavilla, "in the beautiful black veil of a widow." Another critic asserts that it is a mysterious Neapolitan lady whose portrait was painted for Giuliano de Medici, who left the painting in Leonardo's possession so as not to upset his recent bride, Philiberta of Savoy, with a reminder of his former loves. Some have even ventured the hypothesis that the Mona Lisa is the portrait of a man in disguise. In short, a romantic story has been woven around this enigmatic painting. It has inspired writers and poets. Gabriele d'Annunzio, in the tale of *The Man Who Stole the Mona Lisa*, took as a starting point its theft from the Louvre in 1911 by an Italian mason and imagined an "impossible" love. But what are the facts? Actually Vasari wrote only on hearsay and described the painting without ever having seen it. He went on at great length to give a realistic description, not omitting praise for La Gioconda's eyelashes, "which were uncommonly thick." Unfortunately Mona Lisa didn't have any; in those days women shaved their eyelashes. Actually, Mona Lisa is anything but realistic. She is bathed in a liquid atmosphere of muted blue-greens. Behind her opens a dream landscape of mountain peaks, water and mists. These are the elements that make this famous painting the masterpiece of the "sfumato" style—a blending of vague colors and shades to give a misty appearance.

At Leonardo's death, the painting was acquired by Francis I for 4,000 ducats. It remained in the royal collection at Fontainebleau until it was put in the Louvre.

"Mona Lisa" has had an adventurous life. The famous portrait nearly ended up in England when Charles I, an art enthusiast, asked for the hand of Henrietta of France as well as for the painting. But the French objected. Centuries later, on August 21, 1911, an Italian mason, Vincenzo Peruggia, stole the picture to take to Italy. It was found in Florence a few months later and restored to the Louvre.

SIMPLICITY PERSONIFIED

A contemporary of the ornamented ladies painted by Pollaiuolo, Botticelli, Titian, and Raphael, Leonardo's "Mona Lisa" is distinguished by, among other things, the absence of any jewelry. Compared to those ornate portraits, this one is the very model of simplicity. The hair is smooth, lightly covered with a black veil. Her breasts and hands are bare of any jewel. Leonardo always went against the current. This simplicity was characteristic of his private life as well. At a time when men wore long, voluminous clothes, he wore short, rose-colored garments. In an era that was not demanding in matters of cleanliness, he was scrupulously, even maniacally clean. He could not even stand to have paint on his fingers. He took care of his nails, he carefully curled and brushed his beard. It was said that when he was strolling through Florence with a friend one day near the Church of Santa Trinità, he ran into a group of townspeople who were discussing a passage in Dante. Recognizing Leonardo, they begged him to explain the text. At this moment, Michelangelo, disheveled as usual, appeared on the scene. "Michelangelo will explain the verses you are talking about," said Leonardo. "Explain them yourself," Michelangelo retorted. "You who made the model of a bronze horse and could not even cast it." Turning on his heels, Michelangelo left. Leonardo blushed, says his biographer. Blushing was the only instinctive reaction which he never succeeded in controlling. "Patience against insults," Leonardo wrote later, "serves as do clothes against the cold. As the cold increases you must cover yourself with heavier wraps." Leonardo did not hesitate to serve whoever needed his work, and he did it with a prodigious ingenuity. "In due time the King of France came to Milan," Vasari wrote in his biography of the artist, "where Leonardo, having been begged to make something out of the ordinary, made a lion that took a few steps, then opened its chest and showed it to be full of lilies."

In contrast to the richly clad
ladies portrayed by the masters
of the period, the "Mona Lisa"
is notable for the simplicity
of her attire and the total
absence of any ornaments. To
the right of "Mona Lisa" is
"Caterina Cornaro, Queen of
Cyprus" painted in all her
majesty by Titian. Next is the
"Queen of Sheba" in an elaborate
pearl headdress by Bonifacio
Veronese. Below, far left: The
beautiful Simonetta Vespucci
as portrayed by Pollaiuolo,
wearing a snake intertwined with
a necklace on her bare breast.
Next, Simonetta as Botticelli
painted her, with her hair carefully
disheveled. The last one is an
"Unknown Lady" by De Predis,
wearing a beautiful necklace
and a jeweled headdress.

Below: Two drawings by Leonardo. The study for the "Leda," at the left, which is now in the Milan Picture Gallery, and the one for the head of a Madonna, at Windsor, reveal the same mysterious melancholy, faintly relieved by a smile on barely parted lips. Leonardo's life was also a mystery. Left-handed from infancy, he used mirror writing and symbols that are undecipherable to the casual reader. He wrote very little about his private life except to record the moves, occasioned by his work, from one place to another. Art, for him, became an "inner adventure."

Opposite page: The barely perceptible smile of the "Mona Lisa" (above) seems frozen in comparison with "St. Anne's" (below). The smiles on the faces painted by Leonardo are reminiscent of funerary Greek statues or of Gothic statues in medieval cathedrals.

AN
ENIGMATIC
SMILE

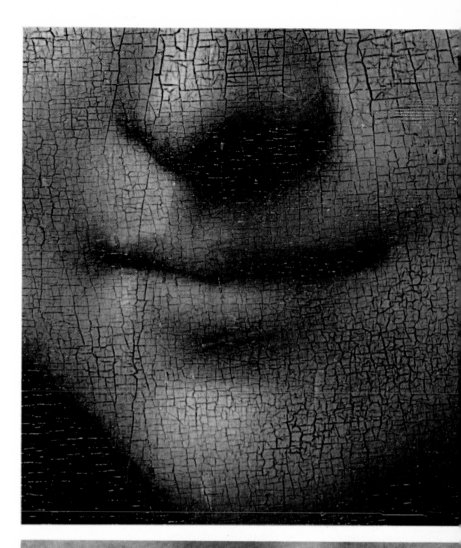

Leonardo could pitilessly record frightful expressions on the faces of wretched old men in the Ghetto. But he could also, with a light touch, hint at the souls of the women who sat for him. Whence came Mona Lisa's mysterious smile? Certainly not from the contraction of muscles; her face is immobile. The smile comes from an inner light that permeates her whole being while barely flickering at the corners of her mouth. Vasari recounts that Leonardo "while he was painting her, had singers and bellringers and buffoons to keep her cheerful and to dispel that gloom that is often present in the painting of portraits—and in this one of Leonardo's there was so pleasant a smile that it was more divine than human to behold." We do not know if the buffoons' jesting really did cause that divinely melancholy smile to dawn on the lips of Mona Lisa. But we do know that Leonardo thought music a stimulus to the senses and to the imagination; so much so that he composed motets and dance arias, and, not satisfied with the musical instruments then in use, invented others: hydraulic organs, or the famous silver lyre with which he introduced himself to Ludovico Sforza. The smiles on Leonardo's subjects also suggest the eternal mystery which enthralled the artist: the mystery of the human spirit, the mystery of sensuality, the mystery of things barely hinted at which fire the imagination. In the *Treatise on Painting* Leonardo speaks, at a certain point, about stains on walls. "You may see in those stains the images of various landscapes, outlines of mountains, rivers, crags, trees, plains, manifold valleys, and hills; you may also see in them battles and lively gestures, strange figures, a quick play of human faces, apparel, and a thousand other things that you will reduce to good and integrated form." In this way he anticipates certain suggestions of the surrealists for whom everything was to become material for fantasy and for creation.

EQUESTRIAN MONUMENTS

In the thirty-page letter in which he introduced himself to Ludovico il Moro, Leonardo spoke only of extraordinary war machines; but in the postscript he added that "in times of peace I think I can equal anyone in architecture . . . or in painting." Leonardo, who wanted to put his own genius at the service of the Duke, knew that a knowledge of wartime engineering was the most persuasive argument. However, he was consumed with a desire to equal and surpass as an artist the great masters of his time, and in particular, Donatello and Verrocchio, who had erected the two imposing equestrian monuments to Gattamelata and to Colleoni. As soon as Ludovico had given him the idea for an equestrian statue of Francesco Sforza, Leonardo threw himself into the study of horses and of various methods of casting bronze. On the occasion of the marriage of Bianca Maria Sforza, sister of Gian Galeazzo, to the Emperor Maximilian, in 1493, a model of the statue was put on display in the courtyard of the ducal palace. Everyone admired it. Leonardo had created "the most gigantic, the most startling, the most glorious masterpiece ever to come from the hands of a man." However, nothing further was done. When the French arrived in Italy with 36 cannons, Ludovico was forced to transform into munitions the seven quintals of bronze destined for Leonardo's statue. This was a hard blow for the artist. Later, after his failure with the "Battle of Anghiari," Leonardo once more had a chance to erect an equestrian statue, one of Marshal Trivulzio, in Milan. At first, Pier Sodrini refused him permission to leave because of a contract that still bound him to Florence; then he conceded a three-months' leave of absence on a 150-florin bail. Leonardo, magnificently welcomed at the court of Charles d'Amboise, Marshal of France, began in the summer of 1508 to draw up a detailed plan for the monument to Trivulzio and to make a series of preparatory drawings. But soon after, the Sforzas returned to Milan and the city was abandoned by the French. With the now unusable portfolio of drawings under his arm, Leonardo, disappointed once more, resumed his travels, this time to Rome.

On these two pages are a series of studies for the never completed monuments. At the top of the opposite page, the one to Trivulzio that was to stand on a columned pedestal. Leonardo was influenced by Donatello's "Gattamelata" (photograph, far left). Above, and to the left: Two studies for the monument to Francesco Sforza, with a charging horse, which recalls Verrocchio's "Colleoni" (opposite page, second photograph). The statue was to have been twenty-two feet high.

The chalk model for the statue of Francesco Sforza, exhibited in the old courtyard of the castle, was seen and admired by Fra Luca Pacioli, among others, who described it in his book "De divina proportione." The long-standing friendship between Pacioli and Leonardo started in 1496. After the defeat of Ludovico, the model, abandoned in the courtyard of the ducal castle, was taken by the Gascons of Francis I, who destroyed it. Only drawings remain to attest to its existence.

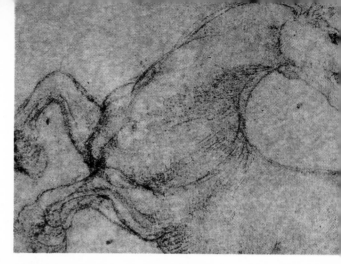

A man of his time, Leonardo liked to ride, and he happily spent many hours during his stays in Milan and in Rome on horses obtained from the stables of the Sforzas and the Pope. He looked upon a horse as a supernatural animal. He had read enough of the classics to know that in mythology the horse had been the mount of the gods, and he saw man on horseback as man made divine, a superman. As soon as he had been commissioned to do the monument to Francesco Sforza, he immersed himself in a study of horses: He wanted to know all about their anatomy, movements, moods, peculiarities, fears and whims.

Opposite page: Two studies of bolting horses for the "Adoration of the Magi." Directly below: A series of drawings for a battle between a horse and a dragon. Bottom of the page: A horse and rider galloping, drawn for the "Battle of Anghiari." (These are all in the Windsor collection.) Leonardo's animal studies were not limited to horses. After the Medusa, which he had painted when he was still a boy, with her hair of snakes and lizards, he portrayed every sort of animal: cats and lions, lap dogs and crabs, oxen and asses, falcons and eagles, ducks and wolves, bats and lambs, as well as the small ermine in the arms of the "Lady with Ermine" in Cracow and the swan in "Leda."

Right: "St. Anne, Virgin and Child," at the Louvre. This is an amplification, in color, with its landscape background and "sfumato" style, of a cartoon that Leonardo made in 1501 and which is now in London. The painting, taken by Leonardo to France, was seen by Cardinal Louis d' Aragon, who had gone to visit the master at the Château de Cloux and who preferred it to the "St. John the Baptist" and the "Mona Lisa." The panel, which measures approximately five feet by four feet, was taken back to Italy by a pupil of Melzi. In 1630 it was at Casale Monferrato where Richelieu acquired it. From then on it became part of the collections of the kings of France. The copy, reproduced below, was done by Salaino and is now at the Uffizi in Florence.

ST. ANNE, VIRGIN AND CHILD

We probably owe the "St. Anne, Virgin and Child" to the modesty of Filippino Lippi, "the gentlest being that ever lived." The story is that he turned down a commission by the Fathers of the Annunciation for an altar painting, suggesting that it be done by a greater artist, Leonardo. In 1500, after the arrival of the French in Milan, Leonardo returned to Florence. He and Salaino were given board and lodging by the Fathers of the Church of the Annunciation, and Leonardo began to plan the composition by means of a cartoon. But he cannot have spent much time on it, for Pietro da Nuvolara wrote in April of 1501, in a letter to the Marchesa of Mantua, Isabella d'Este, that Leonardo "seems to be leading a desultory and unsettled life living from day to day. . . . Since he has been in Florence," Fra Pietro continued, "Leonardo has done only one unfinished sketch, of a Christ child aged about one who, eluding his mother's arms, grasps a small lamb and seems to hug it to himself. He has done nothing else, except to put his hand occasionally to some portraits which two of his assistants were doing. But he is working hard at geometry and is very impatient with the paintbrush." In a letter written the next day, Fra Pietro adds: "In short, his mathematical experiments have distracted him so much from painting that he can no longer stand the paintbrush." Leonardo had succumbed to a passion for mathematics and was devoting most of his time to it. He ignored the pleadings of the Fathers and of Isabella d'Este, who wanted him to paint a portrait of her. Beginning in 1501, da Vinci concentrated on geometry; between 1504 and 1506 he made notes on hydrology, and in 1505 studied solid geometry. In 1510, he was engrossed in the study of anatomy, and wrote papers and carried out experiments on the subject during a stay in Rome. Nonetheless, toward 1510, the "St. Anne, Virgin and Child" appeared to have been worked out at least in its general outline, but remained unfinished. It was to follow Leonardo into France, together with the "Mona Lisa" and the "Virgin of the Rocks."

Opposite page: The famous cartoon for the "St. Anne," which is at the British Museum in London. It measures five feet by three and was drawn in pencil touched over with white lead on brown paper. It was this cartoon that inspired the "Virgin and St. Anne" (reproduced above) of Lund in Switzerland, the property of Professor Lauritz Weibull. Above, right: another Leonardo drawing for the "St. Anne," in the Academy Gallery in Venice. The London cartoon does not correspond to the description by

Pietro da Nuvolara in his letter to Isabella d'Este, although it is faithful to the painting at the Louvre. It is believed, therefore, that Leonardo first did a cartoon in Florence which has since been lost; and that the one reproduced here was done some years later. The latter has been in the hands of a number of owners. For some years it belonged to the Arconati family of Milan, then to the Casnedi family. Later it passed into the hands of the Sagredo family in Venice, who in turn sold

it in 1763 to an Englishman, Robert Udny. In 1791 it was already in the possession of the British Academy. The cartoon also served as a model for a famous panel by Bernardino Luini, which is at the Ambrosiana in Milan. As Leonardo did not complete his painting of "St. Anne" in time for the altar of the Church of the Annunciation, Filippino Lippi returned to the task and started a "Deposition." Perugino finished it in 1506 after Filippino Lippi had died.

Allegory: A boat, with a tree as a mast, and a wolf at the helm, sails toward a globe surmounted by a crowned eagle. The drawing (above), which is at Windsor, was probably made for the wedding of Giuliano de Medici to Philiberta of Savoy. It is another example of Leonardo's taste for the fantastic, which he never lost despite the strong rational core of his temperament. At times he was something of a visionary, as when he described prehistoric times and seas populated with gigantic fish. Right: "Dragon Striking Down a Lion" (at the Uffizi), inspired by his interest in the fantastic.

A STRANGE FASCINATION WITH MAGIC

"It is easy to become a universal man," Leonardo wrote with youthful enthusiasm. But he must have realized that it was not easy to be accepted as such by his contemporaries. His scientific research and his mysterious way of life gained him the dangerous reputation of being a magician. But in what other light could he appear to the men of his time? Leonardo stood apart from the social life of Rome, which appealed so much to Raphael. He used to spend days on end in his laboratory, putting together strange instruments and boiling herbs. He wrote undecipherable cryptograms backward. At night he went to hospitals and dissected corpses. (He boasted of having performed, alone, at least thirty autopsies.) One day, at the order of the Pope, he was forbidden entry to a hospital. Leonardo nevertheless continued to study anatomy with passionate interest because "man is the model of the world." In gathering herbs and distilling their juices, he was seeking a new varnish for his pictures. Among his mysterious instruments were burning mirrors whose destructive potential he wanted to explore.

It was said that Leonardo was often annoyed by his first assistant, Jean des Miroirs (John of the Mirrors), who was trying to steal his secrets and set himself up in competition. Later Leonardo was to complain about his new German mechanic, Georg, who caused all sorts of mischief. Among other things he kept asking for more money, despite their contract, and despite his reluctance to do any work. Then, when Leonardo suggested teaching him Italian, he swore at him in German and stubbornly refused. These domestic irritations were the only things that ever ruffled Leonardo's Olympian calm. Nothing else did—neither the wars of the period, nor the crimes committed by men in power, such as the treacherous Cesare Borgia. Leonardo, with the mind of a scientist, a researcher, looked further than the present. In his writings he lashed out against necromancers and alchemists, perpetrators of fantasies and lies, in order to justify the authentic values of the mind and the truth of scientific research.

The "Allegorical Composition," above, and the "Roaring Lion" at the left (in the Louvre) give us once more the scope of Leonardo's imagination. Without it he would never have been able to invent so many machines centuries ahead of his time. Thanks to his "sacrilegious" dissections, his studies of heartbeats and the working of muscles are still valid today. But Leonardo could also conjure up what he had never seen: he gave a detailed account of the Deluge for the use of diligent young painters; in a letter to the traveler, Benedetto Dei, a forerunner of the modern journalist, he gave a minute description of a giant; and to Diodario di Soria he wrote about the Caucasus as though he himself had visited it.

Perhaps the most curious testimony of Leonardo as a writer is his collection of Fables. They are very brief tales that show a certain Tuscan shrewdness. A few of them are somewhat stilted, while others have freshness and spontaneity, but they all probably reflect Leonardo's style of drawing room conversation. Like other fables, these have a moral. A butterfly is attracted to the brightness of the light and burns itself; the monkey falls in love with a little bird and smothers it with kisses; the ass falls asleep on the ice, melts it and sinks: All the fables reiterate the tragedy of man's ignorance of natural laws. "Oh wretched mortals, open your eyes," is Leonardo's motto.

"OH WRETCHED MORTALS, OPEN YOUR EYES"

THE MOUSE AND THE CAT: The mouse was besieged in his little house by the weasel, who waited with unceasing vigilance to undo him; and from a little hole, the mouse looked out at his great peril. Meanwhile along came the cat who suddenly pounced on the weasel and ate him up all at once. The mouse, sacrificing some of his food to Jupiter, thanked the deity for everything. He left his lair to enjoy his once-lost freedom. He was immediately deprived of it, along with his life, by the fierce teeth and claws of the cat.

WATER: When the water was in the majestic sea it began to want to climb above the air, and, raised by aid of the element of fire into a fine vapor, it seemed to have the lightness of the air. Mounting high, it came to thinner and colder air, where it was abandoned by the fire; and the little granules, being pressed, united and became heavy, whereat pride turned into flight, and the water fell from the heavens; then it was drunk up by the dry earth, where it was shut up for a long time, doing penance for its sin.

THE DOG AND THE FLEA. A dog was sleeping on a sheepskin. One of the dog's fleas, smelling the

odor of the oily wool, decided that this would be a place where he could live a better life than by feeding off the dog. He would also be safe from the dog's teeth and claws. At once he left the dog and went into the thick wool of the sheepskin and began to work into the roots of its hair; but after much effort he found his task hopeless, for the hairs were so thick that they touched, and there was no place for the flea to feast on the skin; after much trouble and toil, he began to wish to go back to the dog, but the dog had gone, and the flea, full of regrets and bitter tears, died of hunger.

THE STONE. A large stone, uncovered by the water, stood on a certain high place, where a pleasant little wood ended at a rocky road. The stone was surrounded by herbs and various flowers of all colors. As it looked at the great number of stones together in the road below, the desire came to it to drop down there, and the stone said to itself: "What am I doing here with these little plants? I want to live with my sisters there." And down it dropped and rolled to a stop among the companions it longed for. Soon it began to be in constant danger from the wheels of the carts, the hoofs of the iron-shod horses, and the travelers' feet. One traveler turned it, another kicked it; sometimes a chip was taken off, or it was covered with mud or the dung of some animal; and it looked back in vain to the place it had left, to that

place of solitude and tranquil peace. This is what happens to those who desire to leave a solitary life to live in cities, among people full of infinite evils.

THE ASS AND THE ICE. A donkey fell asleep on the ice of a deep lake. The heat of his body melted the ice, and the ass sank under the water, woke up, and was immediately drowned.

THE SNOW. A little clump of snow was once caught on the top of a rock hanging from the peak of a very high mountain. Gathering its thoughts, it began to say to itself: "Now shall I not be considered proud and haughty, being in so lofty a place, when I am but a little pinch of snow, and when I realize that all the snow that I can see is lower than I am? Certainly my smallness does not deserve this height, and I know well, as witness my little size, what the sun did to my comrades yesterday, for they were all undone by the sun in a few hours; and this happened because they had placed themselves higher than befitted them. I wish to escape the ire of the sun, and abase myself,

and find a place suited to my littleness."

And throwing itself violently downward, it began the long journey, rolling along from the high mountains and gliding over other snow, and the more it sought lower ground, the more it grew in size, so that when its course finally came to an end on a mound of earth, it was not much smaller than the ground that supported it; and therefore it was the very last patch of snow to be annihilated by the rays of the sun that summer. Let it be said for those that humble themselves: they shall be exalted.

INTEMPERANCE. The unicorn, through its intemperance and its inabil-

ity to control the pleasure it takes in young maidens, forgets its fierce, savage nature and puts all suspicion aside. Approaching a seated maiden, it goes to sleep in her lap, and thus the hunters take it.

FOLLY. Since the wild bull cannot abide the color red, some hunters drape the trunk of a tree in red, and the bull charges at it with great fury and drives his horns into it, and the hunters are able to kill the bull.

THE FLINT AND THE STEEL. The flint, being struck by the steel for a spark, was astonished and said harshly, "What arrogance makes you do this to me? Don't hurt me; you take me for somebody else, for I never did any harm to anyone." To which the steel replied, "If you are patient, you will see what wonderful fruit will come forth from you." At these words the flint was pacified and patiently endured the torment, and gave birth to the wondrous fire whose power operated in an infinite number of ways. This is told for those who take

fear at the beginning of their studies, and then show that they can be masters of themselves and patiently labor, from which marvelous things are seen to result.

THE LILY. The lily placed itself on the bank of the Ticino, and the current tore the bank and the lily.

THE CEDAR. The cedar, proud of its beauty, suspected the plants around it, and had them removed. The cedar, no longer protected by the plants, had its roots torn up by the wind.

THE CRAB. The crab stayed under a rock to catch fish that swam under it. The flood came, bringing rocks that crushed the crab.

A DISQUIETING ST. JOHN

There are two striking aspects to "St. John the Baptist," Leonardo's last painting: the saint's delicate, feminine features, reminiscent of "St. Anne" but with a somewhat disturbing look in his eyes, and the beautiful hand whose tapering index finger points to the sky. The mysterious look of the figure is enhanced by the encircling darkness from which it emerges like an apparition. Here, Leonardo has carried to its utmost limits his technique of "chiaroscuro." The only light which strikes the body of St. John emphasizes his gesture. Some critics have seen in it an echo of French Gothic statues. Actually the figure repeats the gesture of the "St. Anne" in the London cartoon. Hands were one of the great themes of Leonardo. The artist devoted a series of studies to those of the "Mona Lisa," as he had done for those of the angel in the "Virgin of the Rocks." They are delicate and very beautiful. Da Vinci has also left us a sketch of his own hand, its fingers holding a paintbrush. "The weary hand" combines an entomologist's delicate fingers, capable of touching a dragonfly's wings, with a laborer's strength. It was said that had he had only one hand, he could have bent a horseshoe with it. Anything to do with the work of man attracted and interested him. When Leonardo entered the shops of artisans he would question the workers and closely observe the tools of their trade. His first thought was always how to improve their tools, how to simplify man's work.

In order to ruin Pisa, and thereby strengthen Florence, he made plans to build a canal that would divert the course of the Arno River from Pisa. But before starting on the excavation, he invented new types of spades, a new process for erecting scaffolding, a method for waterproofing wood ——abundant work for his "weary hand." During the last years of his life Leonardo's right arm was paralyzed. Cardinal Louis d'Aragon, who paid him a visit, tells of the deep impression made upon him by the sight of this sage, whose majestic bearing and piercing eyes recalled Michelangelo's "Moses."

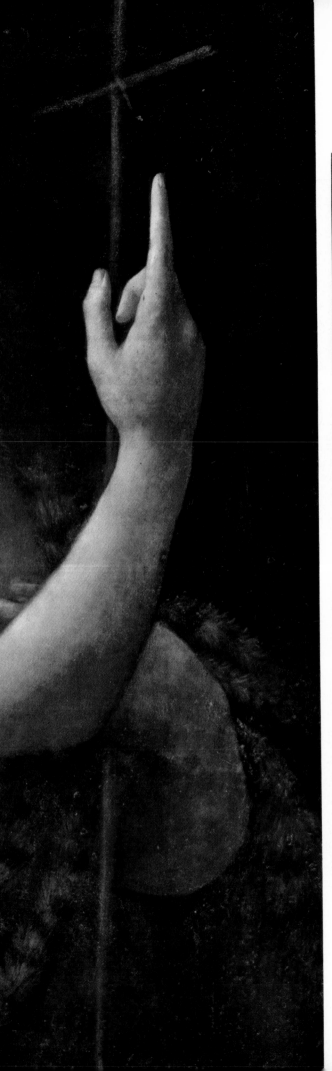

"St. John the Baptist" was painted during Leonardo's second period in Milan—that is, between 1506 and 1513. In 1517 it was seen at the Château de Cloux. It is known that Louis XIII gave it to Charles I of England, but in 1649 the French banker Jabach redeemed it to give to Mazarin. The Cardinal's heirs sold it to Louis XIV. It is now at the Louvre.

This painting, probably the last one from Leonardo's hand, was copied many times by his pupils. From top to bottom, left: "St. John," by Luini, now at the Naples National Museum; next to this is one attributed to da Vinci, which is in the museum at Basle; last: "St. John" in the Pontedera Crastan Collection. Above, the "St. John" in the Cheramy Collection and, last, the one done by Salaino at the Ambrosiana, in Milan.

51

A UNIVERSAL GENIUS

"There is no certainty in science where mathematics cannot be applied," Leonardo wrote. After his meeting with Fra Luca Pacioli, a professor of mathematics, Leonardo eagerly plunged into a study of the subject. But this was only one of a thousand interests of an exceptionally versatile man who richly deserved to be called a "universal man." He was looked upon by his contemporaries as a "very great philosopher." Today we know that he was something more: A scientist attracted by all branches of knowledge. Leonardo questioned everything. "I question" is the expression that occurs most frequently in his notebooks. He questioned others, but especially himself. He reopened the discussion of all the statements made by his predecessors. He accepted nothing blindly. He believed only in direct experimentation, thus anticipating Galileo and Bacon. "Those who want to experiment without possessing some scientific knowledge are like navigators who set sail without a rudder or a compass and who are never sure where they are going." It was this mental outlook that produced the immense bulk of his studies, sketches, and calculations.

NAUTICS
Method of walking on water (above) and
(below) study of a life preserver for keeping its wearer afloat.

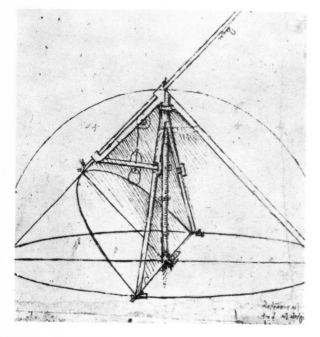

MATHEMATICS
Parabolic compass.

BOTANY
Star of Bethlehem
and spurge

PHYSICS
Diagrams showing
impossibility of
perpetual motion

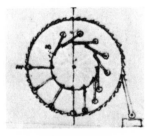

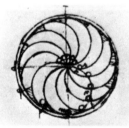

OPTICS
Left: machine for grinding telescopic mirrors
with focal length of nineteen feet.
Right: machine for making
concave mirrors.

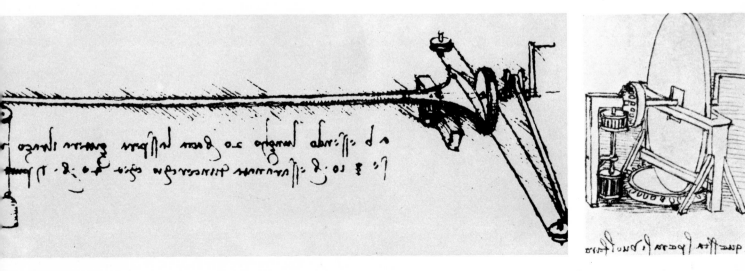

AN INSATIABLE CURIOSITY

Among Leonardo's papers are rough drafts of every conceivable subject: from the art of painting to anatomy and the speed of air; from geological formations to prehistoric remains; from flight to the building of canals. He explored every field of human knowledge. Had his *Treatise on Anatomy* been published it would certainly have contributed to the progress of medical science. Leonardo's "secret weapon" was his keen, untrammeled curiosity. When, on December 29, 1479, one of Giuliano de Medici's assassins was hanged, Leonardo made a detailed drawing of his body and clothing. Later, at the Hospital of Santa Maria Novella, he used to spend hours at the bedside of a man who was nearly 100 years old, listening to the story of his life, covering him with his furs when he saw him shiver in the cold. One day the poor old man died. Leonardo, "in order to ascertain the cause of death," took up instruments and began to dissect the corpse.

ANATOMY
Proportions of man according to Vitruvius.

MACHINERY
Motor with falling weight and ratchet arrangement
with teeth inside wheels.

HYDRAULICS
Well pump

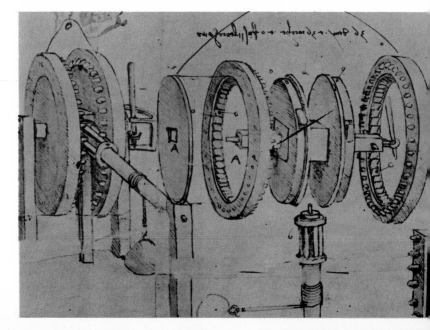

GEOLOGY
Gigantic
explosion

HYDRAULICS
Lock on a canal
used to form
a waterfall.

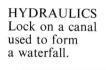

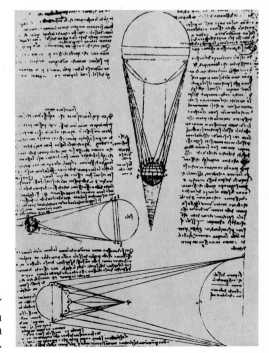

ANATOMY
Muscles of
upper limb.

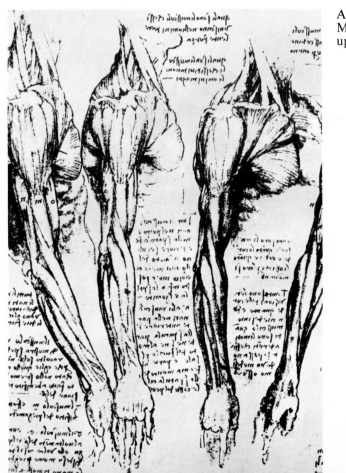

ASTRONOMY
Distance of sun
from earth
and size of moon.

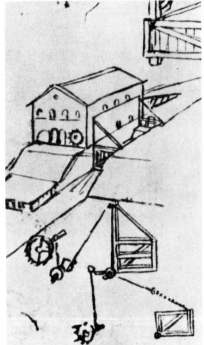

PATRONS
AND PROBLEMS

"I never tire of being useful," said Leonardo. Nor did the men in power at that time tire of making use of his services. The partnership between Leonardo's inventive genius and the practical requirements of lords and rulers, however, did not always produce happy results. The long list of Leonardo's patrons reflects the troubled times and provides a mirror in which to see the vicissitudes of Leonardo's life. He was often constrained to change employers. Lorenzo the Magnificent, who had known him as a boy in Verrocchio's workshop in Florence, was the first to avail himself of his services. From there, Leonardo went on to Milan, with Ludovico il Moro. Their association lasted eighteen turbulent years. Sometimes they were on the best of terms, sometimes not. For example, in 1489, Ludovico decided to cancel the commission for the statue of Francesco Sforza, but the following year, da Vinci noted in his diary: "On April 23, 1490, I began this book and set to work again on the horse . . ." proof that the difficulties had been ironed out. When the French arrived in Milan, Leonardo went into the service of Cesare Borgia, Duke of Valentinois, who sent him as architect and military engineer to inspect the fortresses of his states. His next employer was the Gonfalonier of Florence, Pier Soderini, who tried to use Leonardo during the war against Pisa. After the Florentine episode had ended with mutual dissatisfaction, Leonardo again found himself in Milan, summoned there by the French King's representative, Charles d'Amboise, a great admirer of da Vinci. At the death of Charles d'Amboise, the Sforzas returned to Milan, and Leonardo left for Rome, summoned by Giuliano de Medici. The latter soon died, and his brother, Pope Leo X, another great patron of the arts, could not decide whether to use Leonardo's talents. The last invitation came from the King of France, Francis I. The King welcomed him lavishly at his court and placed the small manor house of Cloux at his disposal. It was said that Francis had so much regard and affection for him that when Leonardo died, after a three-year stay, he died in the arms of the King (a famous painting by Ingres illustrates this touching scene). In actual fact, it was his pupil Melzi who was by his side. Upon receiving news of the great artist's death, the proud sovereign burst into tears.

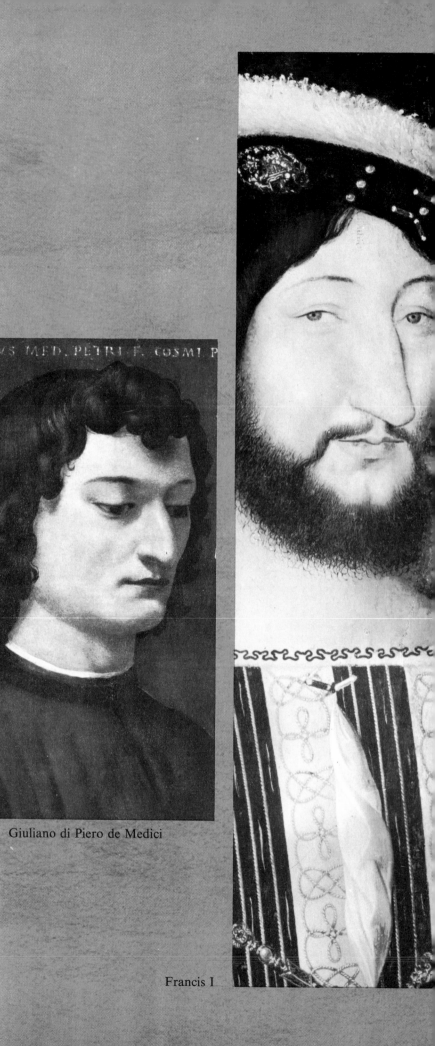

Giuliano di Piero de Medici

Francis I

Ludovico il Moro

Lorenzo the Magnificent

Charles d'Amboise

Cesare Borgia

57

A TECHNOLOGY AHEAD OF ITS TIME

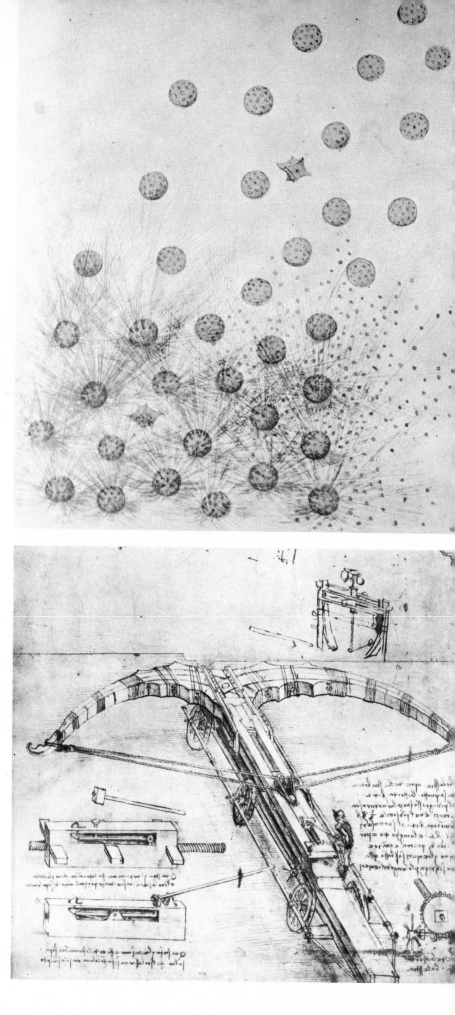

Leonardo was so gentle a man and so full of reverence for every form of life that he used to buy caged birds at the market in order to set them free. Yet at the same time he was passionately interested in military machines for both defense and offense. In this field he evolved methods and processes that were not rediscovered until centuries later. In his famous letter of introduction to Ludovico il Moro, Leonardo catalogued all the things he could do and make, beginning with "very light and strong bridges which can be easily carried, with which to pursue, and sometimes flee from, the enemy; and others safe and indestructible by fire or assault, easy and convenient to transport and place in position. When a place is besieged I know how to cut off water from the trenches and how to construct an infinite variety of bridges, mantlets, and scaling ladders, and other instruments pertaining to sieges. I also have types of mortars that are very convenient and easy to transport," but when "a place cannot be reduced by the method of bombardment, because of either its height or its location, I have methods for destroying any fortress or other stronghold, even if it be founded upon rock." And, as though this were not enough, "if the engagement be at sea, I have many engines of kinds most efficient for offense and defense, and ships that can resist cannons and powder." He also knew how to pass under ditches and rivers through "caves and secret winding passages, made without noise." He had long been interested in the skills connected with military engineering, and studied the writings of others on the subject. When he was at the court of Ludovico, Leonardo had already compiled various studies on the weapons and the fortifications of the castles of the duchy. Later he went to Venice on an exclusively military mission. After having surveyed the entire eastern boundary of the republic, which was threatened by the Turks, he thought up a portable barricade, a movable dike that could be set in place over the Isonzo and Vipacco Rivers to flood or drown attackers. For Cesare Borgia, he made an explosive mixture by combining sulphur, coal and saltpeter to be used as cannon powder. Invited to Florence by Pier Soderini, he made a project to divert the Arno and to flood Pisa (but the project was later abandoned as being too costly). In short, Leonardo was equal to dealing with any problem of military science on land or on sea.

Among the services which he offered the Duke of Milan, Leonardo boasted, were his mortars, "very convenient and easy to transport." With these (see left) he guaranteed "to hurl small stones like a storm, with the smoke of these causing great terror to the enemy, and great loss and confusion." These are the forerunners of shrapnel.
Below, opposite page: Large crossbow on carriage with inclined wheels. This was one of the most intriguing war machines thought up by Leonardo.
Below: Scythed car equipped with flails whirled around by gears on their carriage axles.
Below this: Drawing for an armored car. The covering is made of heavy wooden beams set close together. The gap at the top was used for firing. The drive mechanism was either manual or horse-powered. In this, Leonardo was also centuries ahead of his time. This drawing is at the British Museum.

THE IDEAL CITY

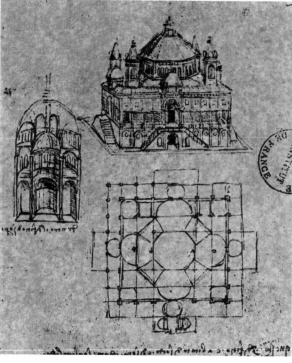

Leonardo's contemporaries must have thought him a perpetually dissatisfied man. Indeed, if we leaf through the hundreds of sheets of projects that he made for dwellings, castles, churches, gardens and canals, we note that he had a mania for altering everything he looked at. But his mania was often based on sound reasoning. Cities, in his day, enclosed within the perimeter of their walls, sheltered thousands of poor devils living in tiny houses in filthy alleys, victims of continual epidemics. It was actually during an outbreak of the plague, which spread through Milan, that Leonardo sketched out plans for an ideal city. He was the first to grasp the necessity for decentralizing the population. As a matter of fact, in his urban planning, Leonardo had thought of segregating the rich from the poor by keeping the nobility within the city and moving the poor out to the country, where, in the healthy air, residential communities would be built for them. The ideal city was to have a checkerboard plan, without walls, to be crisscrossed by a network of canals carrying rapidly moving water. These were to take care of traffic needs, and even more important, the disposal of waste. Elevated roads were planned so that pedestrians could stroll about peacefully while vehicles could circulate unobstructed on the ground. Houses were to be abundantly supplied with galleries and terraces. Leonardo thought up a scheme for cleaning streets and disposing of refuse, showing a foresight which was completely ignored at the time. In France, he dreamed of a canal that would flank the Loire and would go to Lyon; he wanted to drain marshes and swamps; to plant pine trees. He planned a town of wooden collapsible houses on the shores of a river in the open country near Romorantin, to give the poor a chance to lead a better life.

Left: Domed churches with central plans and notes on their measurements. Church architecture was of great interest to Leonardo. With others, he took part in the competition for the building of the dome of the cathedral in Milan, but he withdrew his plans when he learned that Bramante was also competing.
From top to bottom: Two drawings for his ideal city of elevated streets. The first shows the sections of a multistoried palace with a bridge over a canal. The second shows communications and buildings, with many arcades, of a city with raised streets. His ideal city was to be full of gardens, squares and fountains with elaborate waterworks.

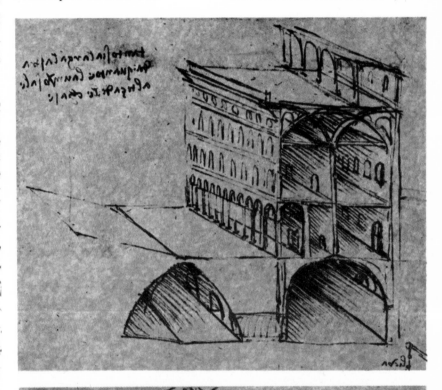

"THE FAMOUS BIRD WILL TAKE FLIGHT"

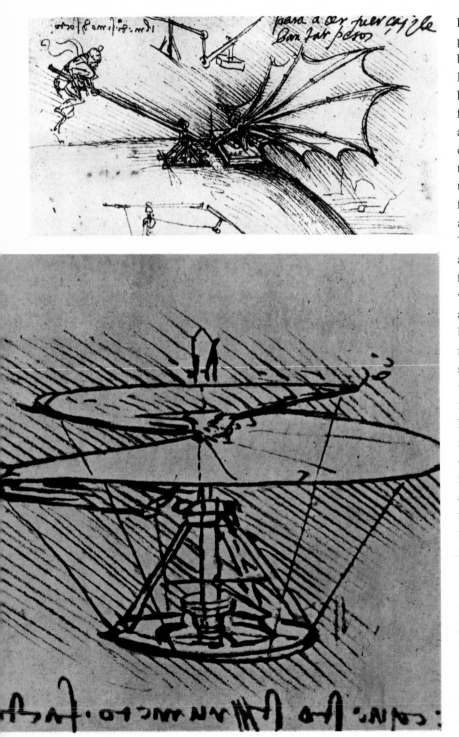

Leonardo devoted a great portion of his life to the problem of flight, for he had always been fascinated by birds, whom he looked upon as the lords of space. He had always dreamed of flying, and hoped to turn himself into a "supernatural" being by imitating the flight of birds. In order to build a machine that would accomplish this, he spent years studying the structure of their wings, the muscles that moved them, the function of their feathers. He filled 18 closely written folios that comprise the *Codex on the Flight of Birds*. This first invention consisted, in the tradition of Icarus, of a pair of wings attached to the shoulders of a man. The wings, formed by a network of wooden nerves and a coating of cloth on which was glued a layer of feathers to increase the resistance to air, were provided with retractable flaps which opened when taking off and closed in landing—all devices that were later to be used on airplanes. But at a certain point, Leonardo realized that man would never be able to achieve the speed and efficacy of birds flapping their wings. Consequently he thought of substituting a mechanical means of flight for the muscular one. He invented a helicopter, or flying screw, and a parachute. He wrote in his notebook: "If a man has a tent made of linen of which the apertures have all been stopped up, and it is 12 ells (27 feet) across and 12 in depth, he will be able to throw himself down from any great height without sustaining any injury." From 1503 to 1506, while living in Fiesole, it appears that Leonardo made a few attempts to fly. In the *Codex on the Flight of Birds*, he wrote, "From Mount Cecere the famous bird will take flight, which will fill the world with its great renown." What did Leonardo mean? Was it a prophecy? According to legend, there was an actual attempt made: Leonardo's machine took off from Monte Cecere, near Fiesole, but it crashed. His pupil, Zoroastro da Peretola, who had agreed to fly it, broke a leg. But there is no record of the failure in da Vinci's notebooks.

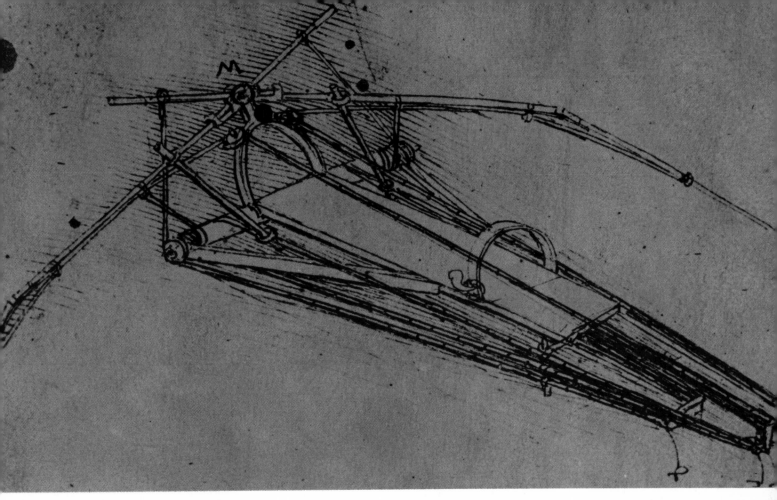

These are the most interesting studies on flight from Leonardo's notebooks. *Opposite page, upper left: A man experimenting on the lifting power of a wing. This was the point of departure of his studies on flight. Below: Leonardo's aerial screw or helicopter, which anticipates the principle of a propeller on a plane.*

Above: One of the first machine models for a man, lying face down with two straps, one for his neck, the other for his waist. The wings were to be moved by the hands on take-off and by the feet on landing. Later Leonardo thought up a more complicated project: The pilot, upright, was to operate the four wings by pushing a pole with his head, turning two cranks with his hands and pressing two pedals with his feet. There were also steps to mount and dismount.

Left: Sketch for a parachute.

Right: Sketches for a slow and controlled landing, inspired by close observation of the flight of birds.

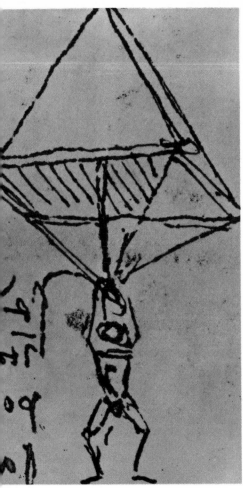

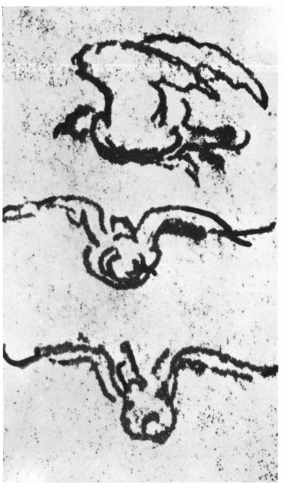

A RELUCTANT GALLANT

In the polished and lively courts which Leonardo frequented he often found himself the center of attraction for some of the most notable ladies of the time. Aware of his genius, they were anxious to achieve immortality by having him paint their portraits. At the court of the Sforzas, during his first stay in Milan, two ladies fought over the position of "first lady": Isabella of Aragon, wife of Gian Galeazzo, the official duke, and Beatrice d'Este, the child-wife of the usurper, Ludovico. It was Beatrice, daughter of Duke Ercola d'Este and sister of the famous Isabella d'Este, who won. Her verve, her elegance, her innate joy of living gradually overcame any pretentions to popularity her rival might have had. Leonardo painted her, covered with jewels, in the famous portrait at the Ambrosiana. The value placed at court on Leonardo's genius is proven by the importance of the festivities he was asked to organize: the famous "paradise festival" for the marriage of Gian Galeazzo and Isabella of Aragon, and, shortly thereafter, the wedding of Ludovico and Beatrice. Leonardo had also done a portrait of the Duke's first mistress, Cecilia Gallerani (thought to be the "Lady With Ermine"). The Duchess fought her rival relentlessly and finally succeeded in having her sent away. Despite his deep affection for his child-wife, Ludovico did not hesitate to take a new mistress and to ask Leonardo to paint a portrait of her. She was Lucrezia Crivelli (thought to be the subject of "La Belle Ferroniere"). Another young lady of the Sforza court who was married off with a great fanfare was Bianca Maria, sister of Gian Galeazzo. At twenty-two, after a series of broken engagements, she married the Hapsburg Emperor Maximilian, bringing him a dowry of 400,000 ducats. For the ladies, Leonardo also did some insignificant bits of work, like the planning of a bathroom for Isabella of Aragon. But another Isabella was impatient to use his services: the Duchess of Mantua. Leonardo promised her a number of paintings but, on arriving in Florence, he promptly forgot the promise. Isabella was one of the most powerful ladies of her time, and yet Leonardo seemed to avoid her. But the ladies did not give up and continued to fight over him. In France, the sister of Francis I, Marguerite d'Angoulême, Queen of Navarre, made innumerable concessions to get him to accept an invitation.

Opposite page: Profile in charcoal of Isabella d'Este, sketched by Leonardo during his brief stay in Milan, for a portrait that was never done. Isabella had married, at fifteen, Duke Francesco Gonzaga. She was the most cultivated woman of her period. She was a patroness of the arts and showed great talent for politics as well.

Below: Leonardo's portrait of the beautiful Cecilia Gallerani, who was for many years Ludovico's mistress. Left, by other artists: Marguerite d'Angoulême, who took special care of Leonardo at the French court. Below this: Bianca Maria Sforza, Ludovico's niece, who married the Hapsburg Emperor Maximilian.

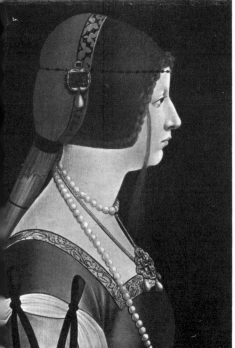

AMBITIOUS PROJECTS
THAT FAILED

Pope Leo X, when he saw Leonardo try out a new varnish before beginning a painting, exclaimed sadly: "Alas, this man will never get anything done because he is already thinking of the end even before he begins." A few years earlier, Pier Soderini had written a verdict even more severe to Charles d'Amboise, who had requested him to send Leonardo to Milan: "Da Vinci has not behaved toward the Republic as he should have, because he accepted a large sum of money and has scarcely begun the great work he was to execute." (Leonardo arranged to leave anyway.) What had happened? Commissioned to do a fresco of the "Battle of Anghiari," the artist had used a type of plaster that he had read about in a book by Pliny, with the result that the work he had barely begun was already irremediably ruined.

At the same time, his project for diverting the course of the Arno, at which 2,000 workers were busy, became the subject of a lawsuit because of an error in calculation. That was not all: The "Last Supper" was being ruined by dampness. The monument to Francesco Sforza remained unfinished. Leonardo failed in those very enterprises from which he had hoped to gain the greatest fame.

The illustrations on these two pages document Leonardo's greatest failures. Left: The figure of the Apostle Philip, in the "Last Supper," is visibly damaged by dampness. Directly below: Sketch for a waterfall on the Arno. The failure of this enterprise caused Pier Soderini to lose faith in Leonardo. Below: Sketch for the equestrian monument to Francesco Sforza, which remained unfinished because of political reasons. In short, none of his major works outlived him, nor were the wonderful undertakings dreamed of or planned by Leonardo successfully concluded. The genius of the builder towered above a world in ruins.

The "Battle of Anghiari" was to have been painted in the Council Hall in Florence, opposite the "Battle of Cascina" by Michelangelo. To give greater relief to the painting and more vividness to the colors, Leonardo, according to Vasari, used an encaustic technique in painting it. The result was disastrous. The colors never dried; the artist then lighted a great fire at the base of the fresco. The lower part dried, but the colors in the upper part hopelessly merged. Had Rubens not copied from Leonardo's cartoon the episode of the standard (opposite page), we should have no trace today of the lost masterpiece. This drawing was engraved by Edelinck.

A GENEROUS TEACHER

No artist was ever less alone than Leonardo; he was generous with his talent, happy to scatter about him the fruits of his inspiration. The De Predis brothers, Boltraffio, Salaino, Marco d'Oggiono and Francesco Melzi lived for years by his side, painting under his direction. Many artists did oil paintings from his drawings and cartoons. Still others, like Bernardino Luini, Cesare da Sesto, and Sodoma assimilated from Leonardo his "sfumato" technique and learned how to make the transition from darkness to full light, yet remained outside the circle of his pupils. Even Raphael took his inspiration from him for the Madonnas he painted between 1505 and 1512. Dürer studied da Vinci with passionate interest. The influence of the ideas and the works of Leonardo made itself felt in Italy as well as in France, Spain, and the Flemish countries, anticipating or, rather, preparing the advent of the baroque and the stylistic richness of the epoch.

Leonardo—who in certain respects was extremely economical, scrupulously noting down every penny spent—behaved with the greatest generosity toward his pupils. He paid them, lodged them, showered them with gifts. During the beginning of his stay in Milan, when he was still short of funds, he was host to Ambrogio De Predis, who lived with his stepbrother Evangelista, a woodcarver, and his deaf-mute brother Cristoforo, a painter of miniatures. Leonardo collaborated with them, and freely gave advice and help. As soon as he had set up his own household he adopted young Salaino and taught him how to paint. He welcomed Boltraffio and valued him without worrying whether the young man's outstanding talent as a painter would make him a rival. Marco d'Oggiono came to Leonardo when he was barely thirteen; he remained ten years. When he met the fifteen-year-old Melzi, Leonardo welcomed him like a son and took him with him wherever he went. In Rome, he arrived with his following—and shared with them his salary of thirty-three gold ducats a month. Francesco Melzi was the only one to follow his master to France.

Opposite page, top:
"Portrait of a Musician"
(possibly Franchino Gaffuri)
formerly attributed to Leonardo
but now thought to be the work
of Ambrogio De Predis
(at the Ambrosiana, in Milan).
Lower left: "Madonna and
Child" by Marco d'Oggiono
(at the Louvre, in Paris).
Lower right: "The Manger"

by Vincenzo Civerchio
(at the Brera Gallery, in Milan)
painted during his Leonardesque
period; he probably met the
master in Brescia and in Milan.
Below: Another collection
of works executed by Leonardo's
pupils. The first is "Susanna"
by Bernardino Luini (Prince
Borromeo Collection, in Milan).
Right: "Madonna and Child"

by G. A. Boltraffio, touched
up by the hand of the master
(at the Poldo-Pezzoli Museum,
in Milan). Lower left: Roxana,
detail of fresco "Marriage of
Roxana and Alexander" by
Sodoma in the Farnesina
Palace, in Rome. Lower right:
"Columbine" by Francesco Melzi
(Van Berbrock Collection,
in Paris).

HARMONY AND ORDER

The geometric patterns on these two pages show the mathematical precision with which Leonardo planned his paintings. Below: The "Last Supper" is arranged to follow a scheme of outward radiation from Christ's right eye, the ideal center of the composition. The "Virgin of the Rocks" on the other hand forms a triangle, the "Mona Lisa," a truncated cone. On the opposite page, an arc seems to enclose the Angel and Mary in the "Annunciation," a youthful work of the artist. Below, left, the "Leda" with her curving form brings to mind a spiral. "St. Jerome" is enclosed within a trapezoid; the "St. Anne, Virgin and Child" are also enclosed in a geometric figure, a pentagon.

Leonardo thought of every branch of knowledge as dovetailing with every other. He believed, for example, that it was through geometry that the principles regulating the composition of a painting were established. It was Fra Luca Pacioli, the mathematician, who had advanced this hypothesis in his *De Divina Proportione* (which, apparently, only echoed the ideas of Piero della Francesca). On the strength of this theory, Leonardo tabulated the proportions of the human body and made geometry the backbone of his paintings. He based all composition on a harmonious scheme, which is illustrated in the reproductions on these two pages: radiation, triangle, truncated cone, arc, trapezoid, spiral, pentagon—all of these enclosing the subject of the picture. Nothing came by chance from his orderly, precise mind. He had a tendency to codify, to classify; his numerous notes for treatises on all manner of subjects attest to this. It was this very scrupulousness in the preparation of his works that later became a source of bitterness and misunderstanding.

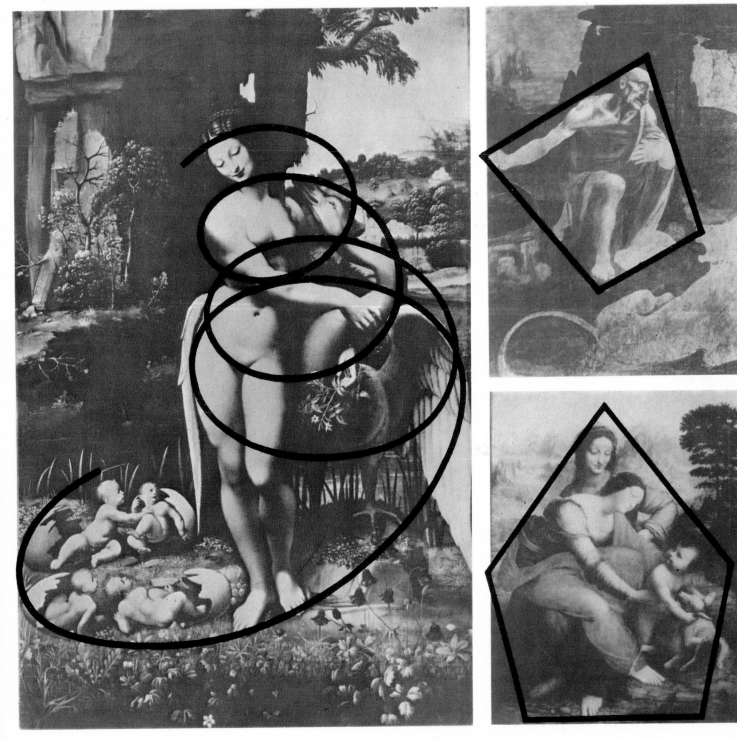

It was during a difficult period of his life, before leaving for Milan in 1482, that Leonardo did this "St. Jerome," which remained unfinished. (It was discovered in 1820 by Cardinal Fesch, who found it in a shoemaker's shop. He had it restored and placed in the Vatican Gallery.) This is the most tragic piece of work by Leonardo, in whose diary can be found traces of the melancholy to which he was frequently prey: "Why do you suffer so?" is written in the margin of the Codex Atlanticus. "The greater one is, the greater grows one's capacity for suffering." And finally the most poignant sentence of all: "I thought I was learning to live; I was only learning to die." This underlying asceticism found its most eloquent pictorial expression in his "St. Jerome."

Although Leonardo da Vinci lived during the full splendor of the Renaissance, he was not a typical man of his time. His rationalism and his desire to limit himself to the possible derive, it is true, from the Renaissance. In most other respects, however, he appears to be a modern man, ready for the daring enterprises that characterize our epoch. The invention of mechanical devices, the conquest of space as well as of the earth, the eagerness to try the untried in every field of human experience—these were his aspirations as well as ours. City planners today could use, to the last detail, his schemes for the building and maintenance of model cities. However, because of his taste for the fantastic, Leonardo remained a man of the Middle Ages. Although he was rational, he was constantly attracted to the irrational in life. He was something of a visionary. When, as an adolescent, he looked into the dark cave in the Apennines, he already seemed to be, symbolically, standing at the threshold of all mysteries. Because of the multiplicity of the interests that spurred him to pursue every field of knowledge, however, Leonardo can be considered, quite rightly, to have been the universal genius par excellence, and with all the disquieting overtones inherent in the term. Man is as uncomfortable today, faced with a genius, as he was in the 16th century. Five centuries have passed, yet we still view Leonardo with awe.

1452—April 15: Born in Archiano, near Vinci, to Piero d'Antonio da Vinci and to Caterina di Piero.

1466—Moves to Florence with his family and enters the shop of Andrea Verrocchio.

1472—Joins the Florentine Guild of Artists. Paints the angel at the left in Verrocchio's "Baptism of Christ."

1473—August 5: First dated drawing of Leonardo.

1478—Commissioned to do an altarpiece for the Chapel of St. Bernard in the Signory Palace.

1481—Commissioned to do an altarpiece for the Church of the Monks of San Donato at Scopeto, near Florence. This is the "Adoration of the Magi," which is to remain unfinished.

1482—Moves to Milan and offers his services to Ludovico il Moro, the ruler of the city, introducing himself as engineer, architect, sculptor and painter.

1483—Signs a contract, with the De Predis brothers, painters in Milan, for an altarpiece for the Fraternity of the Conception in San Francesco Grande.

1485—Ludovico il Moro orders a painting as a gift for the King of Hungary, Mattia Corvino.

1487—Prepares a number of projects for the dome of the Milan Cathedral and makes a wooden model of it.

1490—January 13: *The Paradise Festival*, with scenery and costumes by Leonardo, is presented upon the occasion of the marriage of Isabella of Aragon with Gian Galeazzo Sforza at the Castle of the Sforzas. Summoned to Pavia, along with Francesco di Giorgio and Amadeo, for the planning of the cathedral of this city. July: takes Salaino under his protection.

1491—Prepares a tournament at the request of Galeazzo Sanseverino, for the marriage of Ludovico il Moro with Beatrice d'Este.

1492—Model of the monument to Francesco Sforza exhibited in Milan. According to documents of the period, he is in Rome during this year.

1495—Begins work on "The Last Supper" in the refectory of the monastery of Santa Maria delle Grazie in Milan, a work which is to be finished about four years later. Paints the portrait of Cecilia Gallerani which is known as the "Lady with an Ermine." In the same year he attends a meeting of architects convening in Florence to plan the Council Hall of the Signory Palace.

1498—Decorates the ceiling of the Sala delle Assi in the Sforza Castle in Milan.

1499—After the flight of Ludovico il Moro, he too leaves Milan, occupied by the troops of Louis XII, and moves to Florence.

1500—January – February, sojourn in Mantua at the court of Isabella d'Este, where he does a charcoal drawing of her. In the same year, his presence is mentioned in Venice and in Florence. He prepares the cartoon for the "Virgin and St. Anne."

1502—August 18: Cesare Borgia appoints him military engineer and puts him in charge of inspecting his fortresses in Romagna.

1503—Returns to Florence and is asked by the Gonfalonier, Pier Soderini, to divert the Arno in order to force Pisa to surrender. He is commissioned to do a fresco of the "Battle of Anghiari" for the Council Hall in the Palazzo Vecchio. He starts

the fresco but is forced to interrupt it because of technical difficulties. Rivalry with Michelangelo.

February–April: First studies on the flight of birds. Failure of his flying machine.

1504—Meets with other artists to decide where to locate Michelangelo's "David."

1506—Is summoned by Charles d'Amboise, and leaves Florence for Milan.

1507—Appointed painter and engineer at the court of Louis XII in France. He paints the "Mona Lisa," the "Bacchus," the "Leda," and "St. John the Baptist."

1508—Returning to Florence, he continues his scientific studies. In September he is back in Milan working on hydraulics.

1513—Leaves Milan for Rome and settles in the Belvedere Palace. His patron is Giuliano de Medici, brother of Pope Leo X. At this period his interest is the study of optics.

1515—Leonardo is present at a meeting between Francis I, King of France, Victor of Marignan, and Pope Leo X. He pursues his studies of anatomy.

1516—Death of Giuliano de Medici. He accepts the invitation of the King of France and moves into the manor house of Cloux near Amboise.

1517—Receives the visit of Cardinal Louis of Aragon, to whom he shows his last works.

1518—Prepares the festivities for the christening of the Dauphin and for the marriage of Lorenzo de Medici.

1519—April 25. Dictates his will. May 2: Dies at Cloux and is buried in the cloister of the Church of St. Florentin in Amboise.